This book is presented to:

_____

From:

_____

Date:

_____

A Little Child Shall Lead Them

Story and Illustrations
by John Pomeroy

Written by Greg Perkins

Charisma
KIDS
A STRANG COMPANY

A Little Child Shall Lead Them
by John Pomeroy

Requests for information may be addressed to:

The children's book imprint of Strang Communications Company
600 Rinehart Rd., Lake Mary, FL 32746
www.charismakids.com

Children's Editor: Gwen Ellis
Copyeditor: Jevon Oakman Bolden
Design Director: Mark Poulalion
Designed by Bill Henderson

Library of Congress Control Number 2004116066
International Standard Book Number 1-59185-632-9

05 06 07 08 09 — 987654321

Printed in China

Dedication

To my dear wife, Cami,
whose prayers led me to Christ.

The crowd outside the gate was noisy. They laughed and talked as if they were going to a party. Matthew watched as they inched closer to the wide, wonderful gate. *It must be important,* he thought, *because it's so big.*

It was covered with beautiful carvings and bright colors. Matthew stood on his tip-toes to see what was inside the gate. But he was too short to see in the gate. He couldn't see any balloons or piñatas or cakes or funny hats and steamers. All Matthew could see...were the shadows and darkness in the sky above the gate.

Matthew decided this wasn't any fun at all. He pushed his way out of the crowd. That's when he saw another gate. It was completely different from the big one. This gate was small and simple and unimportant looking.

"Maybe that's why nobody's going inside," Matthew said out loud.

He turned to the crowd and shouted the way he sometimes shouted at his pesky little sister, "Hey, everyone! There's another gate right over here! And there's no pushing or waiting!" But no one heard him. So Matthew shrugged and went to get a better look.

As he got closer, Matthew saw
a man sitting beside the small gate.
He looked nice, but a little sad.

"That must be the gatekeeper,"
Matthew said. "He'll know what's
going on."

"Hi, mister," Matthew said.
"How come no one's using this gate?"

The gatekeeper looked up and
smiled warmly. "Maybe they don't know
about it, Matthew."

"Hey, how do You know my name?"

"Because I know a lot, and I know all about you. I've been waiting for you."

"Who are You?" Matthew asked.

"My name is Jesus, and I want to be your best friend. Would you like to see what's inside My gate?"

Matthew nodded and peeked inside the little gate. His eyes grew wide, and his heart beat fast. It was the most beautiful place he had ever seen! The sky was bluer than any blue. The trees were straighter and greener than any tree on earth. And the street leading to a shiny city in the distance wasn't black like the street he lived on, it sparkled like golden sunshine on water at the end of the day.

"Wow, it's great!" Matthew said, then looked back at the crowd struggling to get into the wide gate. "But why aren't they using this one? It's so much better."

"They don't see it because they don't even believe it's here," Jesus said.

"But how can they miss it! It's as plain as the nose on my face," Matthew said.

"I know," Jesus answered sadly.

They started to go inside when Matthew
stopped. "Jesus, what if they just don't
know about Your gate? Maybe
I should go tell them!"

"That's a great idea, Matthew!" Jesus said and smiled a big, bright grin.

So Matthew ran back to the crowd as fast as his little legs could carry him.

"Hey, hey, everybody, listen!" Matthew said excitedly. "There's another gate right over there." No one paid any attention to the brave little boy.

"Ouch!" he said as someone stepped on his foot.

Matthew yelled out louder than ever, "Listen! There's another gate, and there's no crowding and no pushing or anything!" But no one looked up.

Once again, he tried to get their attention. "It's beautiful inside. Jesus is there. Please come with me," he pleaded, but the crowd just kept marching toward the big gate.

"Ahhh!" he shouted as he was almost knocked over.

Matthew was about to give up, when all of a
sudden a boy struggled out of the crowd…
then a girl holding the hand of her little friend!
Matthew was so excited!

"Hey, do you guys want to go to the other gate with me?" Matthew said. "It's awesome!"

"Yeah, great!" said the boy.

"Oh yes," said the girls, "anything to get out of this noisy, pushy crowd!"

"Well, come on. You can meet Jesus. He'll show us the way inside."

So the small band of boys and girls followed Matthew to the other gate.

Jesus was waiting for them. He smiled big when He saw them coming. "Hello," said Jesus, "are you ready to come with Me?"

They all nodded.

"Can You show us the way?" said Matthew. Then he remembered his manners. "Please?"

"Certainly," said Jesus. Then He bent over and got real close to Matthew. "Matthew, that wasn't easy. I'm proud of you." Then Jesus said to everyone, "Come on, but remember to always stay very close to Me every step of the way."

They agreed. So Matthew and his new friends walked very close to Jesus. They listened to Him carefully and did exactly what He said. And before they knew it, they were standing in the most beautiful place any of them had ever seen.

It was the kingdom of God, where Jesus is with them forever and ever.

Note to Parents

This story of Matthew is based on the parable of the wide gate and the narrow gate. It is a story of hope. No matter what direction the crowd goes, and no matter how your children might be ignored or passed over because they are Christians, they will have a better future than those who never find the narrow gate.

When your child accepts Jesus into his heart, he becomes part of the kingdom of God. This isn't something he has to wait to enjoy when he is old and enters heaven. He can begin to experience God's presence the very day he states his faith. That's a wonderful place for a child to live because it puts God on his side throughout his entire life.